A Note to Parents

DK READERS is a compelling program for beginning readers, designed in conjunction with leading literacy experts, including Dr. Linda Gambrell, Distinguished Professor of Education at Clemson University. Dr. Gambrell has served as President of the National Reading Conference, the College Reading Association, and the International Reading Association.

Beautiful illustrations and superb full-color photographs combine with engaging, easy-to-read stories to offer a fresh approach to each subject in the series. Each DK READER is guaranteed to capture a child's interest while developing his or her reading skills, general knowledge, and love of reading.

The five levels of DK READERS are aimed at different reading abilities, enabling you to choose the books that are exactly right for your child:

Pre-level 1: Learning to read
Level 1: Beginning to read
Level 2: Beginning to read alone
Level 3: Reading alone
Level 4: Proficient readers

D1319256

The "normal" age at which a child begins to read can be anywhere from three to eight years old. Adult participation through the lower levels is very helpful for providing encouragement, discussing storylines, and sounding out unfamiliar words.

No matter which level you select, you can be sure that you are helping your child learn to read, then read to learn!

LONDON, NEW YORK, MUNICH,
MELBOURNE, and DELHI

Series Editor Deborah Lock
U.S. Editor Shannon Beatty
Designer Rosie Levine
Production Editor Sean Daly
Picture Researcher Rob Nunn
Jacket Designer Natalie Godwin

Reading Consultant
Linda Gambrell, Ph.D

First American Edition, 2011
Published in the United States by
DK Publishing
375 Hudson Street, New York, New York 10014

11 12 13 14 15 10 9 8 7 6 5 4 3 2 1
001-182472-August 2011

Published in Great Britain by Dorling Kindersley Limited.

A catalog record for this book is available
from the Library of Congress.

ISBN: 978-0-7566-8930-8 (paperback)
ISBN: 978-0-7566-8931-5 (hardcover)

DK books are available at special discounts when purchased in bulk
for sales promotions, premiums, fund-raising, or educational use.
For details, contact:
DK Publishing Special Markets
375 Hudson Street
New York, New York 10014
SpecialSales@dk.com

Printed and bound in China by L Rex Printing Co., Ltd.

The publisher would like to thank the following for their kind
permission to reproduce their photographs:
a=above, b=below/bottom, c=center, l=left, r=right, t=top

Alamy Images: D. Hurst 18fbr; Nikreates 19bc, 31br; Pegaz 20-21.
Corbis: Heide Benser 26-27; Randy Faris 4; Move Art Management
5. **Getty Images:** Fuse 10t; The Image Bank / John Kelly 19t; The
Image Bank / Martin Poole 16t; Lifesize / Yellow Dog Productions
18c, 32clb; Stockbyte / Steve Wisbauer 18br.

All other images © Dorling Kindersley
For further information see www.dkimages.com

Discover more at
www.dk.com

Contents

DK READERS

LEARNING
pre-level
1
TO READ

My Day

JE My

My day.

PRICE: $2.94 (jfe/m)

DK Publishing

Good morning!
I wake up and stretch.

arm

It's the start
of a new day.

I wash my face
and put on
my clothes.

T-shirt

 clothes

hanger

 breakfast

I sit down to eat my breakfast.

cereal

bowl

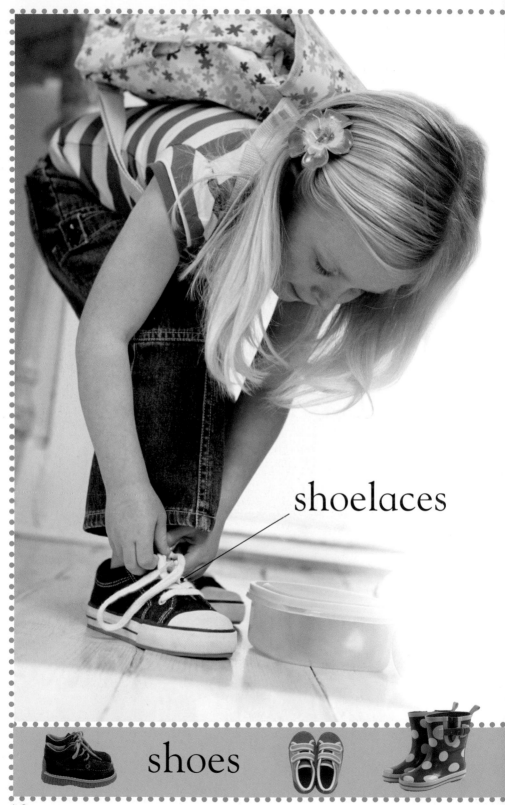

shoelaces

shoes

I put on my shoes
and my coat
for school.

coat

I play with
the shapes at school.

 shapes

square

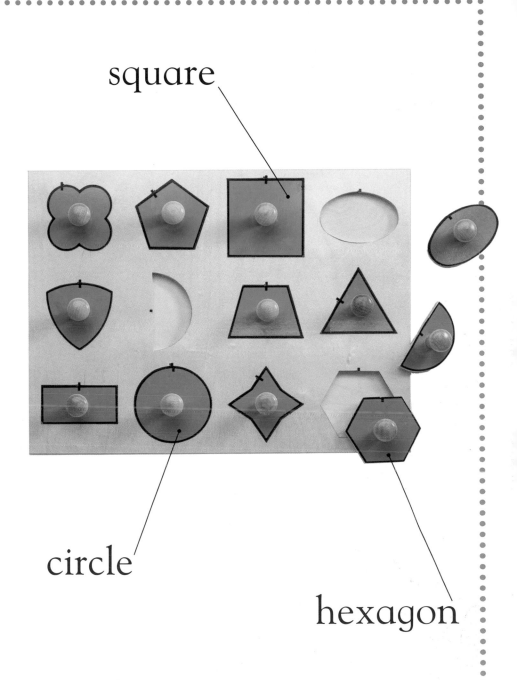

circle

hexagon

 games

I learn games with my class.

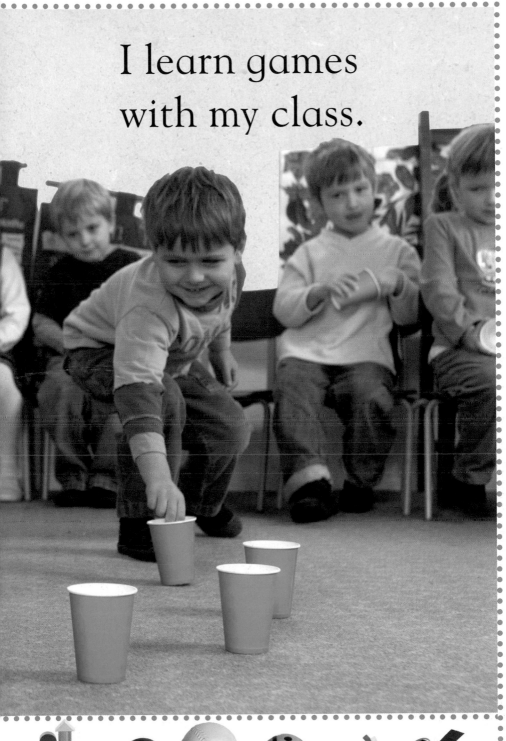

It's lunchtime!

apple

water

I sit down
to eat my lunch.

 lunch

tricycle

playground

I ride and swing and
slide at the playground.

Good afternoon!

 music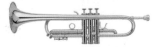

I jump around to music
before I go home.

I play with my toys
when I get home.

train

doll

ball

 toys

peas

  cook

rice

I help
cook dinner.

I take a bath and brush my teeth after eating my dinner.

bathrobe

bathtime

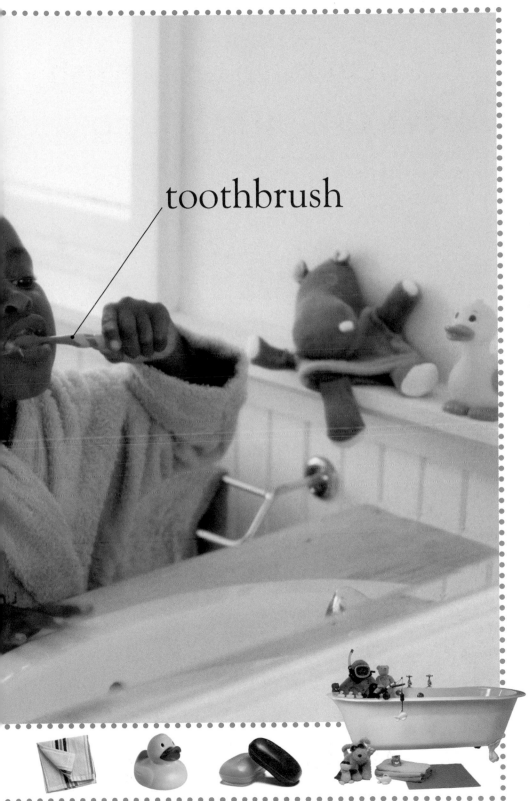

toothbrush

book

 pajamas

I put on my pajamas
and then read a book.

teddy bear

I get into bed.
It's the end of my day.

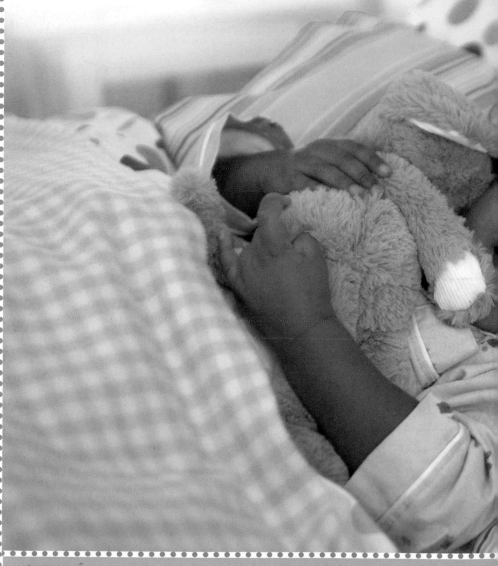

 What did you like

Goodnight!

doing today?

Glossary

Breakfast
is the first meal
of the day.

Cook
is to make food
ready for eating.

Lunch
is a meal eaten in
the middle of the day.

Playground
is an outdoor place
where children play.

School
is a building where
children go to learn.